superstars!
superstars!
superstars!

CREATIVE EDUCATION SPORTS SUPERSTARS

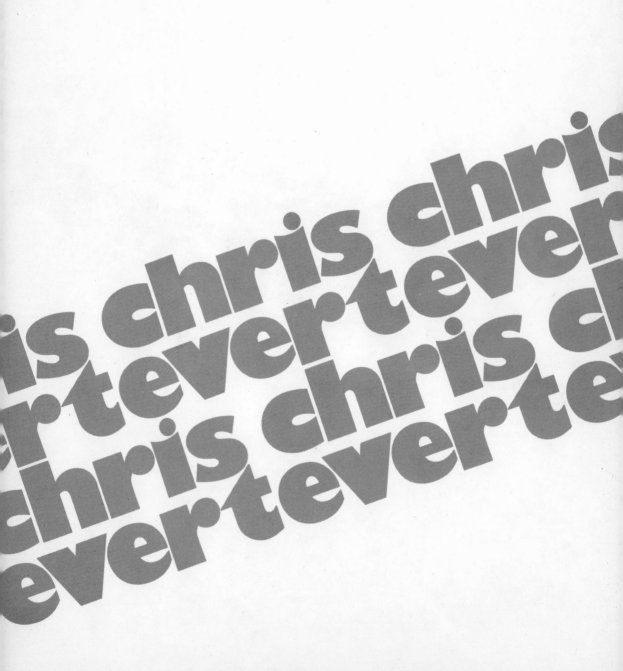

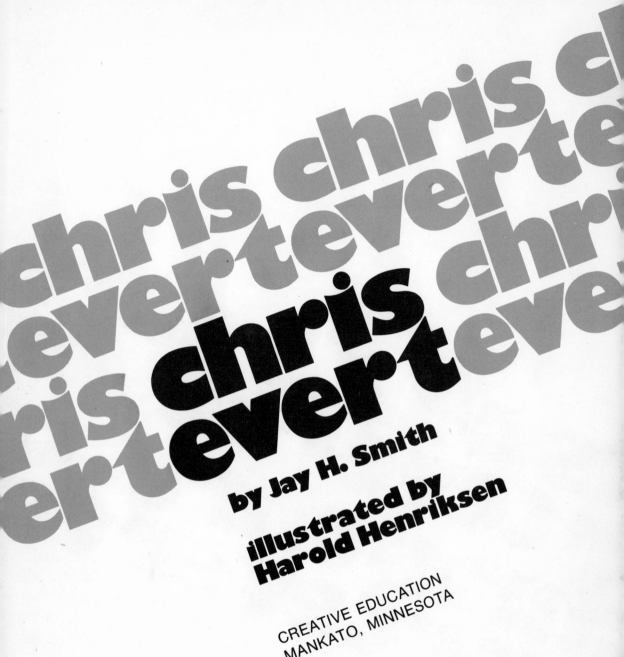

chris evert

by Jay H. Smith

illustrated by
Harold Henriksen

CREATIVE EDUCATION
MANKATO, MINNESOTA

Published by Creative Educational Society, Inc., 123 South Broad Street. Mankato. Minnesota 56001.
Copyright © 1975 by Creative Educational Society, Inc. International copyrights reserved in all countries.
No part of this book may be reproduced in any form without written permission from the publisher.
Printed in the United States.
Distributed by Childrens Press, 1224 West Van Buren Street, Chicago, Illinois 60607.
Library of Congress Number: 75-8739   ISBN: O-87191-439-5

Library of Congress Cataloging in Publication Data

Smith, Jay H.   Chris Evert

SUMMARY: A brief biography of the tennis star who was ranked the number one
woman player in the United States in 1974.

Q. Evert, Chris—Juvenile literature.   2. Tennis—Juvenile literature.
(1. Evert, Chris.   2. Tennis—Biography)   I. Keely, John. II. Title.
GV994.E93S64   796.34'2'0924   75-8739   ISBN O-87191-439-5

3

There was magic in the sunlight of that lovely London summer day. The immaculate grass tennis courts seemed to sparkle like emeralds. Chris Evert felt happy to be back at Wimbledon.

Alone with her thoughts and dreams, Chris smiled nervously. It was amusing and yet painful for the 19-year-old American tennis star to recall the nickname the British press had given her. To them she was the "Ice Dolly."

Some American sportswriters had been even more unkind, referring to her as a "ball machine." Chris knew why she had been given these names. One reason was her seemingly unshakable poise both on and off the court. The other was her highly-disciplined way of playing. No one else in women's tennis could equal her mastery of the mechanical aspects of the game. Like a ball machine, she did have the uncanny ability to return ball after ball with relentless precision and efficiency.

But these nicknames also seemed to imply that she was not quite human, that personally she was mechanical and dull.

Chris was well aware that she could not excite the imagination of tennis fans in the way some of her major rivals could. She didn't play with the emotional fury of a

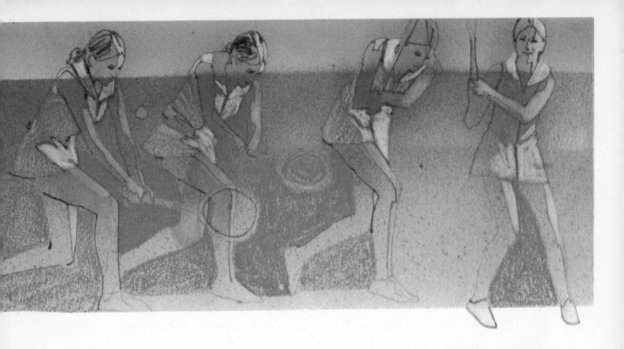

The Cool Disciplined Chris

Margaret Court, the intense passion of a Billie Jean King, or the flowing grace of an Evonne Goolagong.

Unlike these women, Chris hardly ever showed her emotions and rarely the crowd's emotion. The joy of victory and the agony of defeat never seemed to cross her face.

Although Chris had always willingly granted interviews to newsmen, she answered their questions in the same controlled manner in which she played. The graciousness of Margaret, the charm of Evonne, the outspokenness of Billie Jean were not her style at all.

It was her nature to keep her feelings to herself. Essentially shy, Chris wanted to remain a very private person in a world in which the spotlight of public attention always was shining unmercifully upon her.

The few people who knew Chris Evert well understood that she was very different from her public image. "People think she's cold," said Billie Jean, "but really she's a warm human being."

Even though Chris had chosen to conceal her feelings publicly, it still hurt when she realized that most sportswriters and fans thought she had none at all.

But as the opening matches of the 1974 Wimbledon began, Chris had other things on her mind. She was already feeling the nervous excitement that most athletes experience before competing.

For almost as long as she could remember, her one ambition in life was to become the best woman tennis player in the world. Hard work, sacrifice, and uncommon skills had brought her far. But to achieve her goal, Chris knew she must win the Wimbledon championship, the best known tennis tournament in the world.

Chris knew that the experience she had gained in

her first two trips to Wimbledon had been good for her. Both times she had come close to winning the title. In 1972 Chris, then only 17, reached the semifinals, only to lose a dramatic three-set struggle to Australia's Goolagong.

In 1973 she had played even better, going all the way to the finals before losing to five-time champion Billie Jean King. Chris had recorded the most important win of her young career in the 1973 semifinals at Wimbledon, defeating Margaret Court with surprising ease.

All during the first half of the 1974 season Chris had been improving her game, which is based on her superb ground strokes. Her famous two-fisted backhand, which had always seemed to be guided by radar, was even deadlier than ever. Her classic forehand was even more precise and forceful now. Her lob and drop shots, always deceptive and well stroked, were effective weapons.

Chris had added some power and more control to her serve, not her strong point of the game. She had also learned to volley fairly well, if not sensationally. Hitting the ball in the air — a volley — was something Chris had previously done only out of necessity. Now she would even come to the net from time to time.

Two fisted backhand

Her confidence increased as she perfected her skills. The results were soon evident. After losing the final of the Australian Open to Miss Goolagong in January, Chris went on to win five out of eight tournaments on the United States spring pro tour.

Then she went to Europe to compete in the important French and Italian championships. Chris won both of them, protecting her reputation as the best women's clay court player in the world.

Although Chris was practically unbeatable on clay, a slow surface that favors her defensive, backcourt game, she had yet to win a major tournament on grass.

Grass courts, like those at Wimbledon, play fast and produce tricky bounces. They are better suited to the serve-and-volley power game of players like King, Court, and Goolagong.

Although Margaret Court was pregnant and would have to miss the tournament, the 1974 Wimbledon field was strong. Billie Jean King and Evonne Goolagong would be on hand. Chris had never been able to beat either one of them on grass.

When play began, the sunlight had gone. The sky was gray and overcast as Chris took the court in her first match. Second-seeded in the tournament behind Billie Jean, Chris figured to have no trouble at all against unranked Lesley Hunt of Australia.

But Lesley soon made it clear that she was eager and able to pull the upset of the year. She seemed to outplay Chris at every turn in the first set. Lesley forced the set into extra games before Chris managed to win, 8-6. Lesley continued to pound away at the ball and evened the match by taking the second set at 7-5.

Early in the third and final set, Lesley was in command. It seemed only a matter of time before Chris would crumble before the strength of Hunt's quick serves and sharply-angled volleys. Chris needed all her courage to stay in the match. Rallying on every crucial point, she somehow managed to keep her fading hopes alive.

As darkness began to fall slowly over the stadium, Lesley increased her attack. Chris began to lose her cool. "I can't see, I can't see," she called out desperately to the officials. But play was ordered to continue.

Lesley had her chances for victory, but Chris kept

right on struggling, scrambling for every ball. At last the darkness saved her and the third set was halted at 9-9. The two girls would resume the match the following day.

The Evert-Hunt battle had already proved two very important things about Chris. She was an even more fierce competitor than anyone had imagined. She could get upset. She was really human after all.

The following morning, Chris went out to the practice courts with her then boyfriend Jimmy Connors, who had suddenly become one of the world's top-ranked men players. The male pros serve much harder than their women counterparts. Chris practiced returning Jimmy's serve until she felt confident she could handle Lesley's easily.

That afternoon Chris closed out the long first-round match in short order, first winning the game when Lesley was serving — breaking serve — and then holding her own service to win 11-9.

After that, Chris never lost her poise or her concentration on the Wimbledon courts. Nor did she ever come close to losing again in the 1974 tournament.

One by one, the other top players began to feel the intense pressures of Wimbledon. In the fourth round, Rosemary Casals, seeded fourth, was knocked out of the tournament by an unknown — 17-year-old Linky Boshoff of South Africa.

In the quarterfinals, Billie Jean King met the same fate. Unable to serve well that day, she lost her confidence and with it her match to Olga Morozova of the Soviet Union.

Evonne Goolagong was also a quarterfinal victim. A combination of her own lack of concentration and the

OLGA MOROZOVA

LESLEY HUNT

punishing forehands of another Australian, Kerry Melville, proved too much for the third-seeded Evonne to overcome.

There were now four women left in the tournament. Mentally drained by her victory over Evonne, Kerry Melville never seemed to get going in her semifinal match with Chris; Chris moved easily into the finals.

Olga Morozova of the Soviet Union was the other finalist. The Russian had beaten the crowd favorite, Britain's hard-serving Virginia Wade, in the other semifinal match.

A light-hitting clay court specialist, Olga was not figured to do well against the young American star. Olga, however, stormed back to take the match.

Chris was neat and trim as she walked onto the court for the final. Her long, blond ponytail was lustrous and perfectly combed. The mascara, lip gloss, and nail polish she wore had been applied with care. Her tennis dress reflected her quiet manner.

As predicted, Olga didn't have a chance. Chris easily demolished her opponent in only 59 minutes, 6-0, 6-4.

Some fans were disappointed that Chris had not faced a sterner test in the finals, but she was the champion. She had faced a great challenge from Lesley Hunt and had survived, whereas all the others — King, Goolagong, Wade, and Casals — had cracked under the tension.

On the following day, Jimmy Connors provided a storybook finish to Wimbledon by beating Ken Rosewall for the men's title. The British fans were thrilled by the double triumph of Chris and Jimmy, who were then engaged and had announced a wedding date.

Chris headed to Fort Lauderdale, Florida, for a two-week rest. Fort Lauderdale was where it all began. Born

December 21, 1954, Chris is the second of the five children of James and Colette Evert. Tennis was part of the family life. Mr. Evert is the teaching pro at Fort Lauderdale's Holiday Park Tennis Center.

Drew, 21 and a college student, was once the third-ranking junior player in Florida. Younger sister Jeanne, 17, travels with Chris to tournaments and is a promising young player. A younger brother, John, 13, holds a national ranking in his age group. The youngest Evert, Clare, 7, also plays and hits more balls over than into the net.

All of the children began to play tennis at an early age. When Chris was six, her dad saw her hitting balls against a wall. He decided it was time to give her lessons. Chris liked the game and soon began to practice two or three hours a day.

James Evert has been described as a conservative person, a stickler for details. He taught Chris well and she followed a strict training program.

Both Mr. and Mrs. Evert are sensitive to charges that they pushed their children too hard and too fast. Mrs. Evert has said that "The thought of producing tennis champions was the farthest thing from our minds."

Once, angry at such criticism, Mr. Evert said that after he saw how well the children could play, "I wanted to help them become the best they could. If there's something wrong with a father helping his children develop a talent, I'd like to know what it is."

Chris comes quickly to the defense of her father. "I appreciate what my father has done for me," she said at 16. "He is responsible for where I am and most people don't understand.

"Oh, I didn't always like it. When I was in the seventh and eighth grades, I think I missed going to parties. But I've lost interest in things like that."

Chris played in her very first girls' tournament at the age of eight. Four years later she was good enough to be ranked No. 2 in the country in the 12-year-old age bracket. In 1968, she was ranked first in the nation in the 14-year-old division.

But it wasn't until the fall of 1970 that Chris really began to make a name for herself. She had entered the Carolinas Invitational at Charlotte, North Carolina, for the experience. The tournament included some of the world's top women professionals. If Chris was nervous playing against them, she didn't show it.

FATHER &
COACH
JIMMY
EVERT

In her first match she shocked the tennis world by beating Francoise Durr, the former French champion. The next day, 15-year-old Chris upset the great Margaret Court, who had just won the tennis Grand Slam.

After the match with Margaret, Chris burst into tears. "I didn't want to cry," she said, "but when I saw that Laurie Fleming, my best friend and a very good tennis player herself, was crying, I just couldn't help it."

The following spring Chris proved that her victories at Charlotte had not been flukes. By September of 1971, when her star first shone its brightest at Forest Hills, Chris had become an international celebrity.

She spent 1972 playing in amateur and open tournaments. She did not turn professional because the national tennis organization — the United States Lawn Tennis Association (USLTA) — holds that you must be 18 to be a pro. Chris beat the pros often enough in 1972 so that she would have won almost $50,000 if she had been a professional.

Thus, 1973 had been her first year as a professional. Now, a year later, she resumed her winning ways after her success at Wimbledon.

She was particularly devastating in the finals of the U.S. Clay Court Championships. Playing flawlessly, she crushed Gail Chanfreau of France, 6-0, 6-0, in only 15 minutes.

Chris went unbeaten from March 1974 to early September, the time of the U.S. Open Championships. She had won 52 straight matches in 10 tournaments.

The U.S. Open at Forest Hills in New York City was played on grass. Chris, whose reputation was made on clay courts, was still heavily favored to win. She was as impressive as ever in her first three matches, winning quickly and easily. But in the quarterfinals, Chris once again faced Lesley Hunt and the pressure grew.

At first, the two girls seemed to be staging a replay of their Wimbledon match. After the first set was tied at 6-6, Lesley raced ahead 4-1 in the nine-point tiebreaker. She needed only one more point to take the set. But Chris scored four straight points to win the set, 7-6. Disappointed, Lesley lost heart and Chris took the match.

The Forest Hills crowd was almost as disappointed as Lesley. Not only had they cheered for Lesley, they had booed Chris. This had made Chris work hard to maintain

her composure. Later she said, "I'm not used to crowds being against me; maybe Jimmy is, but I'm not."

It was a new experience for Chris, especially because it had happened at Forest Hills. It was here that the Florida native had always been most popular.

Only three years before, a practically unknown 16-year-old amateur named Chrissie Evert had captivated the fans at Forest Hills. Coming from behind in almost every match, she had scored upset after upset before finally losing to Billie Jean in the semifinals of the 1971 U.S. Open.

The crowd had fallen in love with the frail, young girl who fought so hard on every point. They had applauded every move she made and cheered even louder when her opponent made a mistake.

Lesley Hunt had been Chris' quarterfinal rival that year as well. Lesley had seemed headed for victory when Chris had begun to fight back. The crowd had gone wild, upsetting Lesley's concentration. After her loss, Lesley had said bitterly, "I can beat Chrissie Evert, but I can't beat the crowd."

In 1974 the tables were turned. Chris was no longer the underdog that American sports fans love so well. She was an experienced pro who had been so successful that it was difficult for her to again touch the fans' hearts.

Ever since Chris first played Evonne Goolagong at Wimbledon in 1972, tennis fans have come to expect dramatic and beautiful tennis whenever they face each other. And the spectators got everything they hoped for during the 1974 semifinals at Forest Hills.

An Evert-Goolagong match is always something

more than an encounter between two excellent players. (Like Chris, Evonne had captured Wimbledon at the age of 19.) What gives their matches a unique, special flavor is the tremendous contrast in playing style, on-court personality, and appearance between the two girls.

Evonne, who probably has more athletic ability than anyone in women's tennis, plays with effortless instinct. Chris' approach to the game is essentially mental, her style the result of careful study and discipline.

Evonne plays an aggressive, attacking game well suited to her great strength and speed and to her outgoing temperament. Chris, slower on her feet and more fragile, prefers to play defensively, rallying from the base line. Her style, too, is remarkably suited to her quiet, self-inspecting nature.

On the court, Chris is an unmatched craftsman and the more consistent of the two. Evonne, while less predictable, is an artist capable of creating magic.

Dark-skinned, with flashing brown eyes and a glowing smile, Evonne has an exotic beauty that contrasts perfectly with Chris' All-American, blond good looks.

Off the court, the contrast is gone. Both Evonne and

Chris are quiet and shy. Chris and Evonne also have something in common: both of them are champions who play their best when they are behind.

Chris would have her chance to prove that at Forest Hills in 1974. Playing brilliantly, the 24-year-old Australian raced off with the first set, 6-0. Although Chris had not played poorly, she never had a chance.

In the second set Chris began at last to make the match closer, but Evonne was still in control. Ahead 4-2, Evonne now came within one crucial point of breaking Chris' serve. But Chris lifted a beautifully disguised lob over Evonne's head to win the point. Out of immediate danger, Chris held service and won the seventh game.

Then the rains came to Forest Hills, postponing the match for two days. When play resumed, Evonne held her serve for a second set lead of 5-3. Evonne had two match points on Chris' serve in the next game but again Chris managed to escape defeat.

Chris now broke Evonne's strong service twice to even the set at 6-6. After falling behind 1-3 in the tiebreaker, Chris rallied again, taking four straight points. The second set belonged to Chris, 7-6.

At this point, Evonne said later: "I was nervous because, when it gets really tight, Chris can pull out the shots. She is such a determined player you have to concentrate on every shot."

But Evonne got her momentum rolling again and forged ahead 3-0 in the final set. Still refusing to quit, Chris started another comeback. But this time it was too late.

Evonne pushed her lead to 5-3 and served for the match. Trailing 40-love, Chris fought off the first two match points, but couldn't save the third. Evonne wrapped it up with a good volley hit out of Chris' reach.

Although she had wanted very much to win, Chris

took the defeat in stride. She had played extremely well. There was no need to be ashamed.

This was the fourth time in four attempts that Chris had failed to beat Evonne on grass. A month later, Evonne evened the overall match competition between the two young superstars at seven to seven. She beat Chris in the finals of a pro tournament in Los Angeles. First prize was $32,000, the most ever offered in women's competition. The appeal of the young stars, Chris and Evonne, is one important reason for the increased prize money.

Coming up in November 1974 was to be the Evert-Connors wedding. Suddenly, rumors came from Florida that the wedding had been postponed. The Evert family at first denied that the romance had cooled. Soon, however, Chris stopped wearing her engagement ring.

Later, Chris told reporters that now "There are no plans for a wedding." Chris said that both she and Connors were nearing the peak of their careers. "It is an important period for both of us and a chance for us to make the most of it.

"I intend to concentrate on my tennis," Chris said. "I am sure Jimmy does also." Chris pointed out that it would be difficult for them to be together, traveling and playing in different places. They do, she said, "realize how foolish it would have been to go through with the wedding at this time."

There was no wedding, but Chris received an early 20th birthday present before the end of 1974. The USLTA ranked her the No. 1 player in the United States. The top ranked men's player was who else? — Jimmy Connors.

Chris replaced Billie Jean King at the top of the women's list. Billie Jean had been top ranked for four straight years and for seven of the past ten years.

The year had been a good one for the young superstar from Florida. She had won more tournaments than any other woman during the year. She had also won more money — over $250,000. Among the pros on the Virginia Slims tour, Chris had posted the best record for the year, bringing her a trophy as the outstanding player of the year.

She had also done well in tennis's "Grand Slam" — the four big tournaments. These are the French Open, the Australian Open, the tournament at Wimbledon, and the U.S. Open. Chris had won in France and at Wimbledon, had been a finalist in Australia, and a semifinalist at Forest Hills. This record brought her a $35,000 check from a U.S. cosmetics firm for the best overall showing in these events.

Stardom has come quickly to Chris Evert. The tremendous amount of public attention, increased by the romance with Connors, had not all been pleasant. The guidance and support of her family — her father and an uncle represent her business interests — helped her to handle the role of being an internationally known athlete.

Chris is likely to be a tennis superstar for at least another decade. Her success on the court is expected to continue, while it would appear that off the court she will remain modest and soft-spoken. To date Chris has been satisfied to let her disciplined tennis strokes represent her.

Football
Johnny Unitas
Bob Griese
Vince Lombardi
Joe Namath
O. J. Simpson
Fran Tarkenton
Roger Staubach
Alan Page
Larry Csonka
Don Shula
Franco Harris
Terry Bradshaw
Chuck Foreman
Ken Stabler

Baseball
Frank Robinson
Tom Seaver
Jackie Robinson
Johnny Bench
Hank Aaron
Roberto Clemente
Mickey Mantle
Rod Carew
Fred Lynn
Pete Rose

Basketball
Walt Frazier
Kareem Abdul Jabbar
Wilt Chamberlain
Jerry West
Bill Russell
Bill Walton
Bob McAdoo
Julius Erving
John Havlicek
Rick Barry
George McGinnis
Dave Cowens
Pete Maravich

superstars! superstars! superstars! superstars!

CREATIVE EDUCATION SPORTS SUPERSTARS

Golf
Lee Trevino
Jack Nicklaus
Arnold Palmer
Johnny Miller
Kathy Whitworth
Laura Baugh

Miscellaneous
Mark Spitz
Muhammad Ali
Secretariat
Olga Korbut
Evel Knievel
Jean Claude Killy
Janet Lynn
Peggy Fleming
Pelé
Rosi Mittermaier
Sheila Young
Dorothy Hamill
Nadia Comaneci

Hockey
Phil and Tony Esposito
Gordie Howe
Bobby Hull
Bobby Orr

Tennis
Jimmy Connors
Chris Evert
Pancho Gonzales
Evonne Goolagong
Arthur Ashe
Billie Jean King
Stan Smith

Racing
Peter Revson
Jackie Stewart
A.J. Foyt
Richard Petty